Authentic English for Home Science and Allied Sciences

The British Council

Authentic English for Home Science and Allied Sciences

SHYAMALA SIVANANDHAM and S BAGHYALAKSHMI
Department of English
Avinashilingam Institute for Home Science
and Higher Education for Women
Deemed University, Coimbatore

Series Editors
P Ilangovan and David A Hill

Orient Longman

This book and the others in the series are the product of the English for Science and Technology Project set up by the British Council and implemented by them at the Avinashilingam Deemed University for Women, the Tamilnadu Agricultural University, the PSG College of Technology, and the Government College of Technology in Coimbatore, Tamilnadu.

Acknowledgements

The editors and publishers are grateful to the following for the use of copyright material:

Indian Oil Palm Journal for 'Palm Oil for Health and Nutrition'; *Electronics for You* for 'The Spherical Dish Antenna'; U.S.D.A for the table from Handbook 8 of *Composition of Foods*; the Macmillan Company for figures in a table from *Chemistry of Foods and Nutrition*; *The Hindu* for 'Paper-like Blossoms' by O.T. Ravindran and 'Added Risks from Dirty Water'; *Invention Intelligence* for 'Cellular Telephone'; the Ornithological Council for 'A Look at Endocrine Disruptors' from *Issue Briefs*; *Span* magazine for 'Chemicals that Upset Normal Physiological Processes'; *Astronomy Now* for 'Optical Telescopes'.

Every attempt has been made to contact holders of copyright, and sources have been acknowledged at each point where texts appear in the book. The editors and publishers would be glad to hear from copyright holders not listed here to enable them to make due acknowledgement in future editions of the book.

ORIENT LONGMAN PRIVATE LIMITED

Registered Office
3-6-272 Himayatnagar, Hyderabad 500 029 (A.P.), India

Other Offices
Bangalore / Bhopal / Bhubaneshwar / Chennai
Ernakulam / Guwahati / Hyderabad / Jaipur / Kolkata
Lucknow / Mumbai / New Delhi / Patna

ISBN 81 250 2290 2

Typeset by
OSDATA, Hyderabad 500 029

Printed in India at
Orion Printers
Hyderabad 500 004

Published by
Orient Longman Private Limited
3-6-272, Himayatnagar, Hyderabad 500 029

Contents

Note: Teachers' editions will be available on request. Please write to:

Marketing Division
Orient Longman Private Limited
160 Anna Salai, Chennai 600 002

UNIT ONE

Reading

BEFORE YOU READ

A. Work in pairs to do this activity. The scene is the crowded office of a travel agent. 'A' plays the part of the travel agent who is very busy. Typically, people like this do two jobs at the same time—doing their routine work (writing) as well as answering clients' questions. 'B' plays the role of the client. From time to time, A and B come out of their roles to talk about the activity itself.

Do this activity as follows.

- 'A', the travel agent, is busy writing. She can play this part by doing some real copying—the first three sentences of the instruction line above beginning, 'Work in pairs' etc.
  As A writes the first sentence, B as the client asks her three travel questions, for example, 'Are two second-class berths available on the Grand Trunk Express of 15 July?' A continues to write but acknowledges that she is listening to B.
- 'A' finishes copying the three sentences, then comes out of her role to tell B how to ask people questions when they are busy. Likewise, B advises A on how he believes that no matter how busy A is, the client should have total attention.

B. Now read the following text. You will have to do the following AFTER YOU READ tasks in pairs.

1. Decide whose approach was more acceptable—A's or B's.
2. B asks 'A' if she agrees with the point of view of the person in the text. 'A' offers her point of view.

The guest is right.(?) We're wrong.(?)

Leo. J. Fernando

'The guest is always right'. If front office persons work with this attitude, they will surely be successful in their jobs.

The job, of course, calls for a lot of patience and commonsense. Had I not used my presence of mind and a bit of commonsense, I would not have managed to do as well as I have. I would probably have remained a bell captain!

A guest enters the hotel probably with a number of things in his mind. It is an art by itself to understand his mood and react accordingly. If a guest is not in the best of moods, I as a front office person should know how to make pleasant conversation (sometimes maintaining silence may be a better option) with her. It is indeed a very difficult task for a fresher at the job, but it becomes easier as one goes along.

In my ten years of experience in the industry, I have learnt to help every client in the manner he or she would like to be helped, be it the 'pamper-me' person or the leave-me-alone sort.

There are times when I may have to attend to an 'impossible' guest. If he is a valuable client, it is my duty to keep him happy, in spite of his unreasonable behaviour. That's what I'm paid for. And there have been

times when guests have come back to me and apologised for things they have said or done. There have also been many instances when guests have given me a pat on the back for a job well done. Such gestures help me like my job.

I believe I have an aptitude for a job like this in which I have to interact with all sorts of people. That's why I am still in the industry!

(As told to Gloria Suhasini)

[The author, who joined Connemara Hotel ten years ago as a bell captain, is senior duty manager with the same hotel.]

C

AFTER YOU READ

1. Do the tasks listed in B above.
2. Work together to list out some of the qualities a person needs if s(he) wants to take up this kind of job.
3. The writer refers to an 'impossible' guest. List some qualities that make guests impossible in others' eyes.

Writing

BEFORE YOU WRITE

A. 1. Imagine that you come across an advertisement in *The Times of India* for a job that you would like to apply for. List the items that you would have to include in the application, for example, your educational qualifications. Compare your list with someone else's.

2. Work in pairs, A and B. In the text of the letter which follows, select (✓) the appropriate word or phrase.

Now work with another pair, C and D—A with C, and B with D. Compare your choices. Your teacher will help you if you need help.

Letter of application

3 August 2002
The Manager
Harishree Gardens
Mangalore

Dear Sir,

I came to know/understand/realise from the advertisement publish/publishment/published in *The Times of India* from/in/of 8 June 2002 that there is a vacancy for the post of administrative officer in your organisation. Since/Because/For I meet/have/possess the required qualifications, I would like to apply for the post. I enclose my biodata/details about myself/details.

I am confident that I can do my best in the job.

M. Karthika
50 S.R.P. Street
Jayanagar
Bangalore 560 065

B. Work in pairs. Imagine the details and complete the following bio-data. Some parts have been done for you.

Bio-data

	- **M.Karthika**
	- V.Madhusudan
Age:	- 21 years, 3 months
	- Female
Married status	- Unmarried
Permanent address	: 50, S.R.P. Street, Jayanagar, Bangalore 560 002.
	- (080)5625311

- 0091(80)565300
- karthi@vsnl.com

Educational qualifications:

S. No.	Course	University			Subjects studied	Marks/grade obtained
1.	M.B.A.	ADU	1998	I		
2.	B.Com.	ADU	1994	I		

- one year

Details of previous work experience

S. No.			Nature of job	Skills gained
1.	Sony video showroom	6.6.1994 to 24.6.1995		

- (i) Gold medal in corporate accountancy in B.Com
- (ii) Proficiency prize in B.Com
- (iii) Player in the college volleyball team; philately; web designing

I declare that the information given above is true to the best of my knowledge and belief.

: M. Karthika

: 3 July 1998,

: Coimbatore

C. Now work with another pair-team. Compare your responses. Your teacher will help you and will, at the end of the activity, put up the complete bio-data sheet.

AFTER YOU WRITE

Language work

A. Your teacher will now put up the following structures on the board.

- I have... on my form. /What's yours//What do you have?/
- I agree with X. // I disagree with Y, because I think...

Work in pairs to practise them in the ways your teacher suggests.

B. 1. Attempt the following writing task individually.

Follow the conventions in Kartika's letter and write a letter to the managing director of a company in your city stating that you are doing a vocational course, Functional English. As the curriculum requires you to undergo training in a business concern, you are requesting her/him to permit you to undergo training in the company for a period of one month (specify the dates). Mention the fact that you are including a certificate which testifies to your bonafide status as a student of your university.

2. In pairs, look at the first draft of your letter and try and spot any grammatical errors you may have made. These could be spelling, punctuation, subject-verb agreement, movement of adjectives and/or adverbs, the form of the adverb (but not errors of meaning, as they have been spotted and corrected earlier), and so on. Now correct these errors and check whether these errors have been corrected in the second draft.

   Your teacher will display some of the corrected sentences on the board or overhead projector. As a whole class, read and understand the corrections.

3. Continue to work in pairs and compare your letters. Your teacher will offer you help if you need it. Later, after you have had the opportunity to make suggestions to one another, your teacher will display a sample letter on the board. Compare it with yours and make changes after understanding why.

Listening

A. 1. Read the following passage and note down the main points. Your teacher will help you with this. Discuss the gist with a partner. The discussion will help you to understand the passage that you will listen to next.

Palm oil for health and nutrition

Palm oil has excellent health attributes. Some of the findings show that:

Palm oil, like all other types of vegetable oil, is cholesterol-free.

A palm oil diet helps raise the level of good HDL cholesterol and lowers the bad LDL cholesterol.

Palm oil reduces the tendency for blood to clot, thereby reducing the risk of heart disease.

Palm oil is a rich source of beta-carotene, an antioxidant and precursor of vitamin E and tocotrienols (Vitamin E). Red palm oil (RPO) contains 500–700 g/g of tacoferol, 1000 g/g tocotrienols and Vitamin E. Carotenoids in RPO can also serve as powerful antioxidants and anti-cancer agents and are good for the heart.

- Palm oil has powerful antioxidants which keep cancer at bay.
- Solid fats made from palm oil are better for health as they need not go through unhealthy hydrogenation processes.
- It plays a protective role in cellular ageing.

In recent years, palm vitee, a new health product from palm oil has been introduced. Palm vitee, rich in vitamin E, particularly the tocotrienols which act as effective antioxidants in the biological system, may play a protective role in cellular ageing, heart disease and cancer. Palm vitee promises great potential for the marketing of value-added products derived from palm oil.

Considering its positive characteristics and already established wide-ranging benefits, it is hardly surprising that palm oil has progressively gained popularity the world over.

FROM: *INDIAN OIL PALM JOURNAL*, VOL. VI, NO. 31 (MAY–JUNE 1996).

2. Write the gist or summary in your notebooks. Your teacher may ask you to read out some of your summaries.

B. 1. Work with a partner. Listen to a short text on oil supply in the country. Work out the central message of the passage.

2. **Now choose the answer that you think is the gist of this listening passage:**
   a. This is an extract from a general lecture on the topic of demand and supply in economics.
   b. Production of vegetable oils is lower than the demand for these oils in the developing countries.
   c. Vegetable oil is always in short supply in India.
   d. Vegetable oil is always in good supply.

C. Continue to work with your partner and read the passage on the next page. You will then hear the same passage read out.

Underline all those words which you think are different from the ones in the text below. If you would like him/her to, your teacher will read/ play the passage to you more than once.

The passage

The magnitude of imbalance in the demand and supply of vegetable oil as well as the nutritional requirement for the ever-growing population in a developing country like India is eternal. When compared to the developed countries where the per capita consumption of vegetable oil is more than 20 kg., in the Indian subcontinent the availability is only 7 kg per capita, which is far below the world's average and this cannot be increased with the present level of production of the nine annual oil seeds.

Speaking

BEFORE YOU SPEAK

Work in pairs. Use the guide below to role-play the parts of a booking clerk and a passenger.

The 'passenger' can begin the conversation by asking the 'booking clerk' a question.

The booking clerk should answer the passenger's question.

Remember

- ❑ You need to take turns at asking and answering questions.
- ❑ You need to be polite when asking and answering questions.
- ❑ Say 'I beg your pardon?' or 'Pardon me?' when you do not understand what your partner has said.
- ❑ Do not answer with just a 'yes' or 'no.' If the question is, 'Do you want to go to Delhi?' do not just say 'yes' and stop. You can say, for example, 'Yes, I want to travel to Delhi. Which is the fastest train to Delhi?'
- ❑ Allow your partner to also ask and answer questions.

Passenger: (to booking clerk)	Booking Clerk: (to passenger)
Pass: Ask the booking clerk (BC) how many day trains there are from Delhi to Ahmedabad. (*Good morning. Could you tell me…*)	
	BC: Tell the passenger that there are two trains: one starting at night and the other starting in the morning.
Pass: Ask the BC for the departure timings of the trains. (*What are the departure timings…?)*	
	BC: Tell the passenger the departure timings: 7.00 a.m. for the morning train and 3.00 p.m. for the afternoon train.
Pass: Tell the BC that you want a reservation on the afternoon train. (*I'd like a reservation…*or *Could you give me reservation on…, please.)*	
	BC: Ask the passenger how many would be travelling and which class they would like to travel in.
Pass: Tell the BC that two passengers would be travelling by first class a/c two-tier coach and ask how much it would cost.	
	BC: Tell the passenger it would cost Rs 1500, and give the passenger two tickets. (*…Here are your tickets.)*
Pass: Say you are handing over the money and thank the BC. (*Here is the fare, Rs… . Thank you very much.)*	
	BC: Acknowledge the passenger's words of thanks. (*You're welcome.)*

UNIT TWO

Reading

BEFORE YOU READ

A. Work in pairs, A and B, to do this activity.

1. A asks B what her favourite satellite TV channel is. B in turn tells A the name of her favourite channel. B should then ask A if he has also watched that channel. A should respond to B.
2. B now asks A if everyone in their city is able to receive this channel on their TV sets.
3. Now it is the teacher's turn to ask the class a question. The teacher will ask how many of you said 'yes' to B's question (2) and will discuss the answer with you.

B. Continue to work in pairs. B asks A if he knows what the equipment which makes it possible for people to view these channels is called.

C. Now read the following text. Prepare to do the while-reading and after-reading role play tasks in pairs. A is a cable operator. B is an electronics engineer. They should read the text, and ask and answer questions.

The Spherical Dish Antenna

B.N. Kaiwar

A spherical dish antenna, with its distinct advantages over the parabolic dish antenna, may prove to be a more economical proposition for an Indian cable operator.

The majority of dish antennas for satellite TV reception in this country are parabolic types with prime focus feed. This design is efficient as well as elegant to see. However, a parabolic dish antenna (PDA) can serve only one satellite at a time. Any attempt to fit two or more LNBs (low-noise block-down converters) and feed on the same PDA will result in a drastic reduction of signals in all of them.

A SPHERICAL DISH ANTENNA

A personal earth station with a single PDA, LNB and feed requires a motor-driven polar mount and antenna positioner to enable reception from different satellites.

For a cable operator to distribute programmes from different satellites simultaneously, a separate PDA, LNB and feed with a manually adjustable azimuth-elevation mount will be required for each satellite. As there are more than ten satellites visible over the Indian Ocean/Asia Pacific region, programme transmission in this region can be expensive.

Tasks

1. **Discuss the answer: Fitting two or more LNBs on one and the same PDA will result in (a) no reception of the signal (b) the signal reception's becoming weak (c) the signal reception's becoming stronger.**
2. **A should ask B whether it is possible for a cable operator to distribute programmes from various satellites using the same PDA. B should respond to A and then ask A if it would be cost-effective for a cable operator to distribute programmes, using the PDA, from the satellites over the Indian Ocean/Asia Pacific region.**

A spherical dish antenna (SDA) offers some distinct advantages in this respect. The antenna is fixed permanently on the ground (or roof top). An adjustable azimuth-elevation mount is not required. A single spherical dish antenna can receive signals from all satellites within an arc of 20° from its boresight. However, as many LNBs and feeds will be required as the number of satellites to be seen. Each of these will be fixed at different positions and at different heights in front of the SDA, and will point towards the centre of the SDA.

Most PDAs with prime focus feed are designed for an f/d ration (focal length to diameter) of 0.32 to 0.44 (the most commonly used f/d being 0.35 or 0.40). Spherical dish antennas are designed for an f/d of 1.5. Here a different type of feed has to be used instead of the scalar feeds used with PDAs.

A distinct disadvantage is that the LNBs are much further away from the SDA, as compared to PDAs and different LNBs and feeds will have to be fixed at different positions and heights. A much larger area is required to accommodate a single SDA and feeds compared to that for several PDAs.

3. B should ask A to say which—the SDA or PDA—occupies more space.

A single PDA, LNB and feed, with a motor-driven polar mount and antenna positioner, is the best choice for a personal earth station. Further, where space is at a premium, multiple PDA, LNB and feeds with a manually adjustable azimuth-elevation mount are best for a cable operator. However, where space is available at low cost, a single spherical dish antenna with multiple LNB and feeds would be more economical for a cable operator.

From: Electronics for you, *January 1997.*

Writing

BEFORE YOU WRITE

A. Read the following report. Then do tasks A and B which follow.

On-the-job training

A report

Our training was in Anna Achagam. The press was started on 4th August 1995. We started our training on 8th May 1996.

There are several works which are going in the press. These are as follows.

(i)composing (ii) proof reading (iii) proof correction (iv) matter importing (v) machine marking (vi) printing (vii) numbering and (viii) binding.

Proof reading and proof correction are the works related to us. We learned these works. We have to go to the press at 9 o'clock in the morning and we will finish our day's work at 4 pm. We also learned composing matter imposing and binding.

There are three types of bindings. Stiff bound, calico bound corner and leather binding. Matter imposing means letter gathering. That is we have to arrange the letters in order and it will be carried to printing.

As literature students we have to be very careful. First of all we have to do the corrections in the duplicate copy and then give it to the manager. He will check the mistakes corrected and then he will give it for printing.

There are different types of paper sizes. They are

1. double demy 2. double crown 3. double foolscap and 4. code

The ink used for printing are the crold ink and the golden powder.

The machines in the printing press are

1. the foolscap machine 2. cutting machines 3. proof machine and the preacator. The hand press is also used here.

On account of this on-the-job training we benefited a lot. It helped us to improve our language skills.

B. 1. Work in pairs. Read the report again and first identify (underline) the grammatical and other errors in the report. Write the correct forms of the words/phrases on the report, in pencil.

2. Now change partners. A should compare the corrections he has made with the corrections C has made, B and D should look at each other's corrections.

C. 1. In pairs, again, underline all those words and phrases that you think are inappropriately used. Discuss and write down words and phrases in place of the unsuitable ones.

2. Now change partners. A should compare the replacements she has made with C, and B with D.

D. Your teacher will now share a corrected version of the report with you.

Work by yourself. Compare the errors you have corrected with this text. Correct errors you have left out or overlooked.

WRITING

A. Imagine that you are the manager of the printing press. Now draft a report of about 100 words meant for the trainees' head of the institution, referring to the training the students received at the press. Your teacher will help you by

- displaying the starting sentences;
- giving you any words and phrases you may need.

B. Work with a partner. Compare your reports and make corrections if any.

Listening

You will hear a brief extract from a general lecture on Indian science. The tape will be played to you two or three times. As you listen to it for the first time, determine the main point that the speaker is trying to make.

After you have understood the main idea of the lecture, make sure that you understand the details as well.

A. 1. As you listen to the lecture for the first time, determine the main idea of the extract from the lecture. Choose the correct answer from the options presented below:

- ❑ extols the virtues of the ancient Indian art of temple-building
- ❑ provides information on the ancient Indian art of dye-making and weaving
- ❑ lists the sources from which commercially viable dyes can be obtained
- ❑ objectively presents the traditional knowledge base that existed in India.

2. Now determine whether the following statement is true (T) or False (F):

In contemporary India, it is no longer appropriate to say that education and science are for the privileged few. (True/False)

B. As you listen to the lecture the second/third time, list some of the areas in which ancient Indians were knowledgeable. (List out at least four areas.)

Area 1: ____________________ Area 2: ____________________

Area 3: ____________________ Area 4: ____________________

C. As you listen to the lecture the third/fourth time, decide what a visitor would have seen in Kalakshetra in Chennai during Rukmani Arundale's time. (Clue: natural dyes). Complete the following sentence:

A visitor to Kalakshetra during Rukmani Arundale's time would have seen .... varieties .... material. (You need two words before *varieties* and two more words after it)

D. As you listen to the lecture a third/fourth time, focus on a specific piece of information. Complete the following sentence:

The number of different types of plant and animal sources from which extracts for making commercially viable dyes are available is ....

E. Infer the following from the listening passage:

What does the speaker mean by the following statement?

'Science is simply NOT computers and biology.'

Put down your answer here: ....

....

UNIT THREE

Reading

BEFORE YOU READ

Work in pairs to do this activity. Discuss the conditions for good health, and make notes if necessary. For example, there are people who think that only food matters for good health and not exercise.

- A should ask B if he agrees with the statement that exercise, and not something in the food we eat, keeps us healthy and young. B should offer his views.
- B should ask A what a wellknown symptom of vitamin A deficiency is. A should suggest an answer: she may or may not know the answer. Your teacher will note your answers.

Now read the text below and confirm or learn the answer for yourself.

Foods rich in Vitamin A

RECOMMENDED DAILY ALLOWANCE FOR 13–19-YEAR-OLDS (GIRLS AND BOYS): 5,000 UNITS

Names of foods and measures	Units of Vitamin A
VEGETABLES	
Green (cooked 1/2 cup)	
leafy vegetables (kale, turnip greens, collards, mustard greens, spinach, other greens)	10,000
broccoli	2,550
green peas	575
green beans	415
brussels sprouts	260
Yellow	
sweet potatoes (12.5 × 5 × 5 cm)	11,410
carrots, 1/2 cup	9,065

winter squash, yellow, 1/2 cup	6,345
yellow sweet corn (one approx. 12 cm ear)	390
FRUITS	
cantaloupe, 1/2 with 12 cm diameter	6,190
apricots, 1/2 cup, dried cooked	3,450
6 halves, canned	2,475
tomato, 1 medium, raw	1,640
1/2 cup, canned or juice	1,270
orange juice, frozen (180 ml can)	670
prunes, 8–9 cooked	1,105
peaches, raw, 1 medium	880
banana, 1 medium, raw	430
OTHER FOODS	
liver, 4 ounces	60,660
milk, 1 quart	1,560
cheese, Cheddar, 2 cm cube	400
egg, 1 whole	550
butter, 1 tablespoon	460

Cereal grains, dried beans, peas, lentils, nuts, sugars, and some fats contain no or almost no vitamin A.

[Figures in this table are adapted from Handbook 8, Composition of Foods, *U.S.D.A., except that for green leafy vegetables, which is from H.C. Sherman,* Chemistry of Foods and Nutrition, 8th Edition, *New York: The Macmillan Company, 1952].*

How Vitamin A in the diet helps your looks and health

Vitamin A helps general health by its influence on the mucous membrane which lines the mouth, nose, ears, eyes, lungs, digestive and urinary tracts, and glandular organs. Studies have shown that too little vitamin A in the diet results in an increase in respiratory disease, skin, ear and sinus infections and inflammation, and infections of the alimentary tract. On the other hand, when vitamin A is adequate, there is greater resistance to respiratory disease and other types of infection. This vitamin is used in the treatment of tuberculosis.

Vitamin A is important for vision. Sore eyes are found where the diets of families and nations are poor.

In our country most of us get enough vitamin A to prevent serious eye disease. But do your eyes adjust quickly when you go from a lighted street into a dark theatre? Enough vitamin A in the diet helps you adjust quickly from light to dark or the reverse. Our country used this knowledge during World War II. You may have read in your social studies of how flyers were given large amounts of vitamin A so that their eyes could adjust quickly from darkness to light or light to darkness. Vitamin A is just one nutrient working for you with others to help prevent 'night blindness'. Night blindness often causes automobile accidents.

In addition, vitamin A has an important part to play in building strong, good-looking teeth. It helps harden the enamel, and gives the white pearly color which is so attractive.

One of the first things that happens in experimental animals and in persons under observation when vitamin A is too low is a change in the skin and hair. As you progress in this study, you will learn that other nutrients, or the absence of them, also affect the quality of the skin and hair. When vitamin A is deficient, the hair becomes drier and coarse. Little 'goose pimples' may form around the elbow. Blackheads, whiteheads, and pimples appear, especially across the back of the shoulders and at places where hair grows out of the skin. When vitamin A is increased in the diet sufficiently, these symptoms disappear. You can see then that the cream and butter which you eat may do more for your skin than the cream you rub on it.

Delayed effect of too little vitamin A in the diet

If food could talk, it would tell us what it can do for us—and it does, through our health and appearance. But we have to understand the sign language that food 'speaks.' This requires time and study. For example, it was found that when twin animals had the same diet through two generations except that one had whole milk and the other had skim, it made a difference in their health, appearance and length of life. At first the animals grew equally well, and looked equally attractive. But the animal on skim milk was getting much less vitamin A, and when the reserves stored in his body were used up, his hair began to look rough. This was even more noticeable in the second generation. The animals on a good diet except for vitamin A could not grow normally; their coat of hair was much rougher, and they were unable to produce and nurse healthy babies.

When vitamin A was doubled in the normal basic diet, the animals looked better, and lived longer. Then four times as much vitamin A was added to the basic diet, and the health record and length of life were further improved.

This study tells us that we cannot always see the immediate value of a good diet, or the harm of a poor one. It takes time for food habits to show their good or ill effect on us.

WORDS TO WORK WITH

international units: the 'measuring stick' for vitamin A and vitamin D, instead of weight.

carotene (kærəti:n): a substance in green and yellow plants from which the animal body can make vitamin A.

mucous membrane (mju:kəs): tissue lining body cavities such as the nose, ears, mouth, and digestive and urinary tracts.

FROM: MILK AND MILK PRODUCTS, *PP 44–6.*

AFTER YOU READ

1. Work by yourself. Make a note of what foods you think you should eat in order to get your daily requirement of 5,000 units of vitamin A. When you write out the diet that you prefer, you should remember to include a variety of foods in various quantities.
2. Now work with a partner. A should ask B why in the experiment with the twin animals the hair of one of the animals began to look rough. B should respond, and then ask A to say when this change took place, since both the animals looked healthy at the beginning.
3. Have you found the answer to question 2 in 'Before you Read'? If you have not, read the text once more to look for the answer.

Writing

BEFORE YOU WRITE

A. Work in pairs, A and B, to do the following activities.

1. List some of the experiments that you have carried out recently in the laboratory. If you had to describe some of them to others, how would you present the information in writing? Think about this and make notes. At the end of this part of the activity, the teacher will present a possible format for experiments. Copy the format and proceed to question 2.
2. **Discuss the following with a partner and make notes:**
   a. Is information easier to process when it is presented in textual form than if it is in tabular form?
   b. What do you think are the separate advantages of these two methods of presenting information?
   c. Does the nature of information we aim to get from an experiment influence the choice between presenting information in tabular form and in textual form?
3. Now, change partners. A should compare her responses with D, and B with C. Your teacher will help you if required. S(he) will ask a few students to read out their list of experiments. S(he) will then go through the discussions you had in the 'Before you Write' activity and comment on these. Your teacher will also elicit the responses of the class to the discussions in task (1) above.

   Prepare to do the writing task which follows.

WRITING

A. Read the texts, in tabular form, of the following reports. Then do task B which follows.

1. Kovac's test
2. the Ehrlich–Boehme test
3. Gore's test
4. the Gnezda test
5. the methyl red test
6. the Voges–Prosakauer test
7. Werkman's test
8. the modified O'Meara's test
9. the standard Barritt's method

IMVIC test

Aim : To observe the presence of E. coli and A. aerogenes by IMVIC test.

Principle : E. coli and A. aerogenes are normally referred to as faecal and non-faecal contaminants of water respectively and are the most important organisms of the coli form groups, since they closely resemble each other in their morphological and cultural characteristics. Biochemical tests performed to differentiate them are collectively designated the IMVIC test reactions.

Reagents

1. KOVAC'S REAGENT
   Dissolve 5 g of paradimethyl amino benzaldehyde in 75 ml of amylalcohol and add 25 ml of conc. HCL.

2. THE EHRLICH–BOEHME TEST
   Solution I : To 1 g of paradimethyl amino benzaldehyde in 95 ml 95% ethyl alcohol, add 20 ml of conc. HCL.

   Solution II : Saturated aqueous solution of potassium persulphate.

3. PREPARATION OF METHYL RED SOLUTION
   Dissolve 0.1 g of bactomethyl red in 300 ml of 95% alcohol and made up to 500 ml with distilled water.

4. THE PREPARATION OF THE MRVP MEDIUM
   Buffered peptone 7 g   Bactodextrose 5 g
   Dipotassium phosphate 5 g   Distilled water 1 l
   Adjust pH to 6.9.

Sterilise in the autoclave for 15 min at 1 lb or 121° C.

Procedure	Observation	Inference
1. **Kovac's test** To about 5ml of the 24h culture of the organism is added 0.2 or 0.3 ml of Kovac's reagent.	i. the solution turns dark red ii. the solution turns yellow	indicates the presence of indole produced from faecal contamination of E.coli by tryptophan indicates the absence of indole
2. **Ehrlich–Boehme test** To about 10 ml of the culture is added ethyl ether. This is shaken well and then solution I is added along the sides of the test tube.	the interface of the two liquids turns purplish-red within 5 min	indicates the presence of indole
To about 10 ml of the culture is added 5 ml of solution I and then 5 ml of solution II and is shaken well.	the solution turns red within 5 min	indicates the presence of indole
3. **Gore's test** The cotton plug used for plugging the culture tube is moistened with 4 to 6 drops of solution II and then with the same measure of solution I. The plug is replaced in the tube and is pushed down until it is at about the surface of the culture. The tube is heated in a boiling water bath for 15 min without allowing the medium to touch the plug.	the plug begins to appear red	indicates the presence of indole

Procedure	Observation	Inference
4. **Gnezda test** A dry filter paper containing the saturated oxalic acid is introduced into the culture.	it turns pink	indicates the presence of indole
5. **The methyl red test** To 5 ml of the culture is added 5 drops of methyl red solution.	it turns a distinct red	indicates the presence of acid produced by the E. coli forms
	it turns yellow	indicates the absence of coli forms and presence of A. aerogenes
6. **Voges–Prosakauer test** To 5 ml of culture is added 5 ml of 10% solution of potassium hydroxide and mixed well. This is allowed to stand exposed to the air and is observed at intervals of 2, 12 and 24 hrs.	an eosin pink develops	The colour is found to be due to the presence of acetyl-methyl carbinol (3-hydroxy–2-butanone) from dextrose by aerogenes.
7. **Werkman's test** 2 drops of 2% solution of ferric chloride are added to 5 ml of 10% sodium hydroxide and the contents are shaken well.	a stable copper tinge appears for a few min	The colour is found to be due to the presence of acetyl-methyl carbinol (3-hydroxy–2-butanone) from dextrose by aerogenes.
8. **Modified O'Meara's test** A few drops of 25 mg creatine in 40 per cent potassium hydroxide are added to 5 ml of culture and 5 ml of 40% KOH (or NaOH)	it turns a stable red within a few min	The colour is found to be due to the presence of acetyl-methyl carbinol (3-hydroxy–2-butanone)from dextrose by aerogenes.

Procedure	Observation	Inference
9. Standard Barritt's method 0.6 ml of 5% naphthol in ethyl alcohol and 0.2 ml of 40% KOH are added to 1 ml of culture.	it turns a stable red within a few min	The colour is found to be due to the presence of acetyl-methyl-carbinol (3-hydroxy–2-butanone) from dextrose by aerogenes.

1. **Kovac's test**
   To about 5 ml of the 24h culture of the organism was added 0.2 or 0.3 ml of Kovac's reagent. It turned a dark red, indicating the presence of indole produced due to faecal contamination of E. coli by tryptophan. Yellow indicates the absence of indole.

2. **the Ehrlich–Boehme test**
   To about 10 ml of the culture was added ethyl ether. This was shaken well and solution I was added along the sides of the test tube. The interface of the two liquids became purplish red in 5 minutes indicating the presence of indole.

   To about 10 ml of the culture was added 5 ml of solution I and then 5 ml of solution II. This was shaken well. It turned red in 5 minutes indicating the presence of indole.

3. **Gore's test**
   The cotton plug plugging the culture tube was moistened with 4 to 6 drops of solution II and then with the same amount of solution I. The plug began to appear red, indicating the presence of indole.

Sample: Tabular Presentation for Gram's Method of Staining (see summary on pages 35–36)

Procedure	Observation	Inference
A drop of the culture was transferred onto a clean dry glass slide, the smear was allowed to dry in air and	i. a violet stain appears	indicates the presence of gram-positive bacteria
then fixed by passing it once or twice through a flame stained with methyl violet for 1 minute. The excess stain was	ii. it turns pink	indicates the presence of gram-negative bacteria and other tissue cells

poured away and then the stain was fixed with Lugol's iodine solution which was allowed to act for 1 minute. The iodine was washed away with alcohol till no more colour was seen. This was counter-stained with carbol fuchsin for 20 seconds. It was then washed in a gentle stream of water and dried between the folds of a blotting paper. It was then examined under the oil-immersion objective.		

B. Work by yourself. You have read the summaries of the Kovac's test, the Ehrlich–Boehme test and Gore's test on page 25. Now transform any three of the other tests from tabular format to summary format in the same way: the IMVIC, the Gnezda, the methyl red, the Voges-Prosakauer, the Werkman's, the modified O'Meara's and the standard Barritt's tests.

AFTER YOU WRITE

A. Work with a partner. Compare your summaries, seek help from your teacher if necessary and make corrections in the facts. Now look at the summaries on page 25 and make any changes you may need to make in the language and style of presentation. Your teacher will help you.

B. Work in pairs. Write out tables for your experiments as under question A 1 of 'Before you Write'. Compare them with the ones on pages 23–25. Make changes or corrections, if necessary. If there are many corrections to be made, produce a second draft of your table. You could also look at the table for Gram's Method on pages 25–26 and compare yours. The teacher will help if required.

C.

Language work

Work either by yourself or with a partner. Practise the following written structures in 'Gram's Method of Staining' above. Work out similar structures for a cooking activity that you can think of, for example, making an omelette.

A drop of the culture was transferred onto a clean dry glass slide.

The smear was allowed to dry in the air.

The teacher will ask you to report on how you presented the method of making the omelette. Use the laboratory style of writing reports for this purpose.

D. You have described the making of an omelette in the laboratory format. Now write it as you would a recipe. First, list all the ingredients that you will need for the omelette. Then write the step-by-step procedure that has to be followed to make an omelette. For example:

Take the eggs and whip them with a beater or a fork.

Your teacher will ask a few of you to read out your recipes to the class and will also make corrections if necessary. S(he)will also request the rest of the class to read the report and to speak out or write their comments on it.

Listening

A. Work with a partner and listen to the tape. You will listen to a text. As you listen to the tape for the first time, make quick short notes on the text. Use the notes below to guide you on the notes.

1. Is the passage about ecology or population?
2. What does the lecturer mean by 'ecology of population interaction'?
3. Is it about the interaction between different people in society?
4. Is it about the interaction between plants and animals?

B. Now listen to the tape again. Mark the following statements True (T) or False (F).

1. An intra-specific relationship is concerned with different species. ( )
2. An inter-specific relationship is concerned with the same species. ( )
3. An Inter-specific relationship can be classified into two types. ( )
4. Successful survival depends on the closeness of the associations. ( )
5. Antagonism includes parasitism and competition. ( )

C. Complete the table below.

classification	beneficiary	host
commensalism parasitism	remora sea anemone	

D. What do you understand by the term 'predation'? Write a definition of the word and suggest a few examples to illustrate the term. Your answer should not exceed 50 words. Your teacher will play the tape again if necessary.

E. What kind of ecology of population interaction do lichens show?

Write your answer here: ______ ________________ .

Speaking

A. Work in groups of three or four for this activity. Imagine a situation where you have come home from college (you usually stay at the hostel) and found the house locked (although you had already written to your family to say you would be coming home that weekend). Discuss all possible modes of action that you could take to resolve your doubts about what happened to your family and why there is no one at home to receive you.

Remember: In any discussion, you need to say your part and must then allow the other members of the group to say their parts too. It is a good idea to pick up what someone in the group has said and to use it as a link when your turn comes (for example, *What Suman said was true, but...*).

Here are some points to use in the discussion:

- asking the neighbours
- looking for the key in its usual place (for example, on top of the door, below the stack of newspapers on the rack, with the neighbours, with your cousin who lives on the next floor, in your grandparents' house two streets away)
- looking through the windows
- knocking on the door or calling out in a loud voice
- waiting patiently for the family to come back from wherever they had gone
- getting alarmed and thinking of calling up the emergency police control room
- getting alarmed and start thinking of calling up the nearby hospital (where one of your parents was admitted for an emergency operation some months ago)
- looking into the mailbox to see if your letter had arrived by then
- looking around to see if that day's newspaper has been taken in and looking for other signs of the usual activity suggesting that everything was normal with the family and that they had just gone out to the local cinema or were visiting a friend/relative.

B. In small groups of three or four, study the information on the bougainvillea plant presented in the form of a table on page 31. The plant is common in cities and towns and in some villages as well. You may have seen this common plant but you may not have known all these facts about it.

This information has been culled from a newspaper article (titled 'Paper-like blossoms', by O. T. Ravindran. Your task is to make sense of the tabular information given on page 31 and make an oral presentation at the end of the group discussion. In order to prepare for the presentation, make notes under the different headings as you discuss the subject. Compare the qualities of the bougainvillea with those of other flowering plants. You can also contrast a few of the qualities of the bougainvillea with those of other flowering plants.

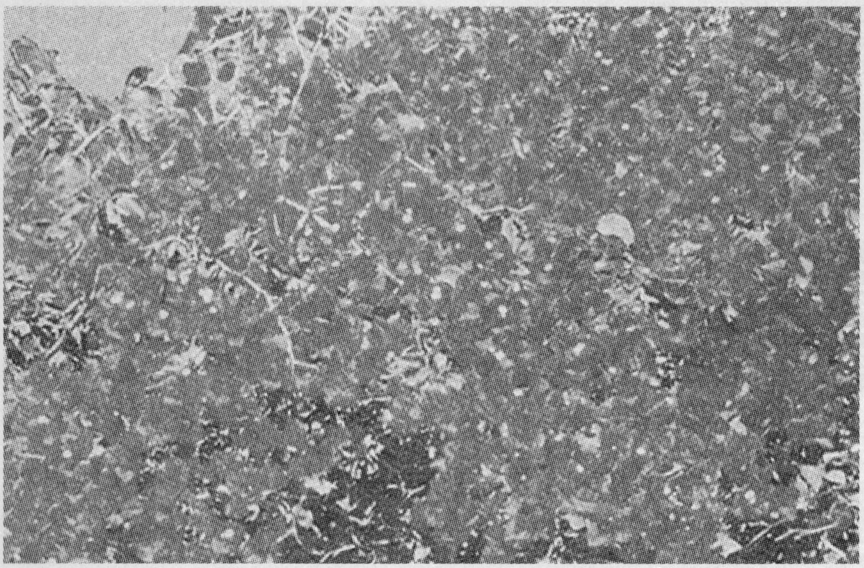

C. A member of each group will now do the presentation. Her or his task will be to use the notes that the group has put together and to make a brief presentation of not more than two minutes to the class. The presentation should be as close to the original text as possible, should emphasise the important points and should leave out details which are not necessary. The presentation will be assessed on the basis of clarity, systematic ordering and sequencing of facts and on the member's completing the presentation in the two minutes allotted.

Some facts about the bougainvillea

common names and species names	flowers and bracts	history and place of origin	propagation	factors for growth	growth and formation
multibracted bougainvilleas	*real flowers*: insiginificant	*bougainvilleas are native to*:	*easy to grow*	*needs:*	
bougainvillea mahara (= dark crimson)	small and tubular	the tropical South and Central America	grow in the wild	They need good sunlight.	They require pruning, shaping.
bougainvillea roseville or 'Roseville's delight' (= golden orange)	attractive part of plant: the modified bracts	named after: Louis Antoine Compte de Bougainville	propagated by cuttings, layering and budding	They dislike water-logging.	They require manure.
bougainvillea cherry blossom (= white suffused with purple)	In other plants, the bracts are small and leaf-like.	He was the celebrated 18th Century Admiral and the first Frenchman to cross the Pacific.	rarely propagated through seeds		They grow in the wild as large climbers using curved thorns.
bougainvillea pink champagne (= light purple)	bracts are large, brightly coloured and papery in texture.	One of the islands of the Solomon islands now part of Papua New Guinea also bears his name.	The plants in the garden are not true species but hybrids and varieties.		They grow in gardens as climbers on lawns and hedges.
The above varieties evolved from 3 species: 1. bougainvillea spectabilis 2. bougainvillea peruviana glabra 3. hybrid: bougain-villea buttiana	thorns arise from above the auxiliary buds on the branches. multibracted bougainvilleas: bracts are smaller produce attractive inflorescence	Camerson, accompany-ing the admiral, collected the first bougainvillea from Brazil.	New cultivars are produced by crossing the plants among themselves.		

UNIT FOUR

Reading

BEFORE YOU READ

Work in pairs and do the following activities.

1. Find out whether it is possible to talk to someone over the telephone in a moving car.
2. Determine whether this instrument is called a pager.

The Cellular Telephone

M.L. Bala

In the fast-changing scenario of communications, dramatic changes have taken place over the decade in the operations of mobile communications. Mobile communication has been in vogue right from the early days of the invention of radio-telephony and caters to the specialised needs of fire brigades, police, defence and other essential services.

Most of the pre-cellular mobile telephone systems had certain inherent constraints. These constraints were created, for example, by the use of high power transmitters, the small number of channels, and co-channel and adjacent channel interference. The next logical step in the evolution of mobile communications was 'cellular technology' which has grown at a fast rate over the past ten years.

The basic philosophy of the cellular system in the Public Land Mobile Network (PLMN) is as follows:

- Divide the entire service area into smaller ones called cells.
- Use low power base stations to serve the area of each cell.
- Use low power mobile subscriber units to operate within the cell.
- Call processing tasks are divided between mobile subscriber units;.
- Use high-speed common channel signalling between base stations and the mobile.
- Reuse the channel subject to certain basic principles. This enables optimal utilisation of the frequency spectrum.
- Handing over calls between one base station to another is possible when the mobile vehicle passes from one region to another region. This makes it possible for the service to be extended to larger areas (Fig. 1).

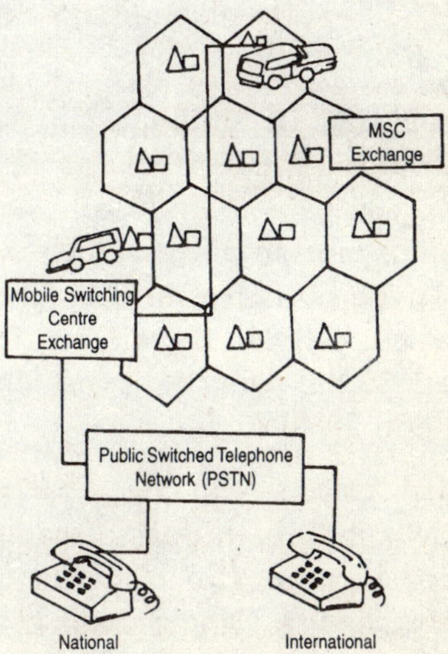

THE MOBILE SWITCHING CENTRE (FIG. 1)

The Cellular Environment

In any typical cellular environment, the communication between the cell site and mobile is via many paths. In fact, the direct path between the transmitter and the receiver is usually obstructed by buildings, trees and other objects. At UHF, the mode of propagation of the em wave from the transmitter to the receiver is largely by way of scattering, either

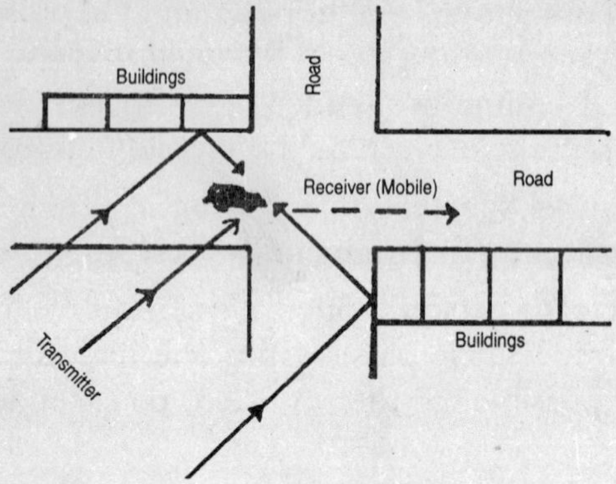

A MULTIPATH PROGAGATION MODEL (FIG. 2)

by reflection from the flat sides of buildings or by diffusion around people-made or natural obstructions (Fig. 2).

In urban areas with a cluster of buildings, the signal received by the mobile at any time would consist of a large number of horizontally travelling plane waves whose amplitude, phase and angle of arrival relative to the direction of motion of the vehicle would be random. The phase and the spatial angle of arrival of each component of the wave can be regarded as statistically independent. The random electrical phase of the received signal can be considered to be uniformly distributed between 0 and 2p (360°).

Two types of adverse effects can be observed due to cellular surroundings. The first is multipath due to scatter or reflections from surrounding obstructions within 100 ft of the moving vehicle. This gives rise to a short-term fading. The second is the shadowing of the direct line of sight path producing slow variations of the mean received signal strength. This produces long-term field strength variations. In a typical cellular environment, the received signal will show fading that consists of rapid fluctuations around the mean signal level varying slowly as the vehicle moves from one location to the other.

FROM: INVENTION INTELLIGENCE, *JANUARY 1997.*

AFTER YOU READ

A. 1. Work in pairs. A should tell B briefly how the cellular telephone works. B should make up for any omissions A makes, correct the mistakes, and generally support A's attempts at telling.

2. A should now ask B to tell him or her about the problems pre-cellular mobile telephone systems faced. B should respond and, in turn, ask A to say how the cellular system services large areas.

3. Discuss how signals received by the mobile unit travel.

4. Discuss what causes 'multipath'.

B. Work as a whole class. Your teacher will ask you to say what answers you considered in 2, 3 and 4 above. This can be followed by a discussion in which the whole class participates with comments and help from the teacher.

Writing

BEFORE YOU WRITE

Work in pairs and complete the following tasks. Your teacher will help you if you need help. Read about Gram's method of staining bacteria below, with the aim of a) listing the different types of bacteria that are differentiated using this method and b) listing the different types of reagents that stain the bacteria.

Gram's method of staining

Aim

To differentiate bacteria into two principal groups: gram positive and gram negative

Principle

The procedure involves the use of at least three chemical reagents that are applied sequentially to a heat-fixed smear. The first reagent called a primary stain must be crystal violet or another type of pararosaline dye. The reagent imparts colour to all the cells. A mordant, Gram's iodine increases the affinity between the primary stain and the reactive substances in the cell. As a result a crystal violet-iodine complex (CV–I) is formed inside the cells. A decolourising agent is a good lipid solvent and a good dehydrating agent. Following decolorisation a counter-stain is used that counteracts with a deep blue violet of the stained-gram-positive cells. Basic fuchsin or safframine or red dyes are commonly used as counter-stains.

Materials

a – young culture organism; staining solutions **b** – dissolve crystal violet (dissolve 2 gm of crystal violet in 20 ml 95 per cent alcohol) and 0.8 mg of ammonium oxalate in 80 ml distilled water. Mix the two (a and b) in Lugol's iodine/Lugol's solution (dissolve 1 gm iodine and 2 gm KI (potassium iodide) in 300 ml distilled water); 95% ethanol, dilute carbol fuchsin (1:20) or safframine (0.5 %).

Procedure

Transfer a drop of the culture onto a clean dry glass-slide. Allow the smear to dry in the air and then fix it by passing it once or twice through the flame. Now stain with methyl violet for a minute. Pour away the excess stain and then fix the stain with Lugol's iodine solution which should be allowed 1 minute to act. Wash the iodine with alcohol and continue washing it until no more colour can be removed. Counter-stain with carbol fuchsin for 20 seconds., then wash in a gentle stream of water. Dry between the folds of a blotting paper and examine it under the oil immersion objective. Gram positive bacteria take up the violet stain and gram negative bacteria and other tissue cells take up the counter stain and appear pink.

Discussion

Gram positive cells stain blue-violet in because they retain the primary stain, crystal violet. On decolorisation with alcohol the CV-I complex from the cell wall does not get removed because of the presence of low lipid content. The gram negative cells with alcohol lose the CV-I complex on decolorisation. Hence these cells take up the secondary stain carbol fuchsin and appear light red.

WRITING

Work in pairs, A and B. Look at the information in 'procedure' in the text you have just read. Convert the information into a table. Now give your table to another pair-team, C and D, and take the table prepared by them. Now convert the table before you into text form again. Your teacher will monitor the work and may ask some of you to read the material prepared.

AFTER YOU WRITE

Compare the table you have prepared with a similar table on Gram's Method of Staining on pages 25–26 of Unit 3. Make any necessary corrections in yours and draw up a second draft of the table. The teacher will check your work and offer help if necessary. Your teacher may also ask some of you to read your reports out aloud in the class and will correct mistakes, if any.

Listening

BEFORE YOU LISTEN

A. 1. Work in pairs. You might have seen that some South Indians are strikingly different from others. They have a far lighter skin colour and hair, blue eyes and are tall whereas generally South Indians are not so. Discuss why this might be so and go on to discuss whether such people will have progeny like themselves.

2. Work in small groups of three or four to discuss this. In the animal world there are some animals that do not look like other animals of the same species at all. A case in point is the zebra without stripes. Why does this happen to some zebras?

B. Work in pairs and follow the steps mentioned below.

- You will hear a lecture on mutation. As you listen to it for the first time, determine the purpose of the lecture.
- Try and listen to the tape without asking for it to be stopped, the first time. This will help you to understand the general purpose of the lecture (the gist).

- After you understand the gist of the lecture, make sure that you understand the details of the lecture. To help you do this you can ask for the tape to be played two or three more times.
- As you listen, make sure that you make notes of the different types of mutation that are referred to in the lecture.

LISTENING

A. Choose the correct answer. The lecture that you are listening to is about

1. the harmful effects of mutation
2. the different types of mutagens in nature
3. the structure of the nucleotide
4. the different types of mutation

B. Determine the technical term given to the agent that causes mutations. Choose the correct answer from the following options:

1. purine
2. mutagen
3. pyrimidine
4. DNA sequence

Write your answer here: __________________.

C. As you listen to the lecture for the second time, listen to the definition of mutation. Now complete the following sentence which defines mutation:

Mutation is any change brought about in the base ________ _____________ of the __________________.

D. Work in pairs. Listen to the lecture a third time. The boxes below are already labelled. They are the two different types of mutation: spontaneous and induced mutation. As you listen to the lecture a second or third time, write the essential characteristics of both spontaneous as well as induced mutation, in the table on the next page:

SPONTANEOUS MUTATION	INDUCED MUTATION
a. ________________ ________________ ________________	b. ________________ ________________ ________________

(**Keywords**: exposure/natural/artificial/mutagens)

E. Continue to work in pairs. Here is a list of items. As you listen to the lecture again, mark and circle the items which are physical mutagens.

1. mustard gas
2. x-rays
3. nitrous acid
4. colchicine
5. temperature
6. gamma rays
7. formaldehyde
8. alpha rays
9. beta rays
10. UV rays
11. infra-red rays

F. Here is a list of mutation-inducing agents. With the help of a friend, find out what kind of agents they are. You can ask your teacher to play the tape yet another time.

LIST: transposons, retroviruses and mutator phages

Write your answer here: ________________.

G. Listen this time for specific information. Complete the sentences below.

1. What is the definition of 'mutation rate'?

   Mutation rate is ____.

2. What is mutation frequency?

   Mutation frequency is ____.

   Missense mutation is ____.

AFTER YOU LISTEN

A. In pairs list the different types of mutation that you came across in the lecture.

1. ______________________________________.
2. ______________________________________.
3. ______________________________________.
4. ______________________________________.
5. ______________________________________.
6. ______________________________________.
7. ______________________________________.
8. ______________________________________.
9. ______________________________________.
10. ______________________________________.
11. ______________________________________.
12. ______________________________________.
13. ______________________________________.
14. ______________________________________.

B. In small groups determine what would happen if an aminoacid sequence is altered in the genes of a living organism.

Speaking

Activity 1

BEFORE YOU SPEAK

With the help of a partner read the extract of an article on the next page. The article is about environmental contaminants that affect normal physiological processes in animals. After you read the article, you will study a table which provides the names of specific chemicals and their effects on certain animals.

Make notes as you read this extract. Your notes should be brief and clear. They need not be in full sentences. Compare your notes with your partner's notes.

A look at endocrine disruptors: assessing the threat of hormone-disrupting environmental contaminants to birds

Introduction

Many environmental contaminants of human origin have the potential to act like hormones or to interfere with hormone action. These contaminants are often referred to as 'endocrine disruptors.' Chemicals of very different types, including industrial chemicals like PCBs, insecticides such as DDT, common pesticides, and many fungicides, can act in this way.

These chemicals have the potential to interfere with the development of sexual and reproductive structures in embryos and young birds. During early life stages of all vertebrates, including birds, hormones permanently influence the development of the reproductive tract and the brain, notably those areas that control reproductive behavior. An alteration or disruption in the development of these reproductive structures may become evident only after the bird grows into an adult and cannot breed properly. Disruption of hormonal action by these contaminants in adult birds can cause a change in reproductive function, especially if the bird is exposed to the chemical during the breeding season. However, in contrast to the exposure of an embryo, a single exposure to an adult bird is unlikely to cause permanent harm.

What is known about this problem? What is 'endocrine disruption'?

Endocrine disruption refers to the interference or alteration, by environmental contaminants, of the hormonal signals that control normal physiological function in animals. This mode of action is not a new discovery. There is abundant published evidence for changes in hormone levels in adult organisms upon exposure to such compounds, which may be environmental contaminants or naturally occurring chemicals. What is new for wildlife toxicology is the emphasis on the permanent effects of endocrine-disrupting contaminants on embryonic development and the recognition of the long delay after exposure until the appearance of an effect. In addition, proponents of the importance of this mechanism point to the variety of chemicals of human origin that are known to have endocrine effects. Not all endocrine-active compounds necessarily alter normal function of the animal, but we have good information on this for only a handful of these chemicals.

Does endocrine disruption occur in wild birds?

We do not know, but we suspect it does. There is good experimental evidence from hatchling gulls that were exposed to DDE (a metabolite of the pesticide DDT) that was injected into their eggs. These birds developed abnormal gonads that were more like ovaries than testes in some respects. It is not known how these physical changes seen in embryos might affect the later reproductive capability of these birds.

The information from studies on bird populations in the wild is more equivocal, in part because effects cannot be attributed with certainty to contaminants acting through a hormonal mechanism. Numerous studies correlate hormonal changes in affected birds with changes in breeding behaviour or reproductive success, but the data so far do not establish endocrine disruption as the ultimate cause. In fact, very few studies have looked for endocrine disruption specifically in wild bird populations. Studies that have found a correlation between increased contaminants and changes in breeding behavior or reproductive success include:

- female-female pairings in Western gulls off the California coast during the late 1960s and early 1970s; this phenomenon declined when DDT contamination of the local environment declined
- the drop in population levels of gulls, terns, cormorants and eagles (all fish-eaters), breeding on the Great Lakes and a subsequent increase in population levels after the use of organochlorines ended
- thinner eggshells produced in many birds exposed to DDT.

Issue Brief from the Ornithological Council, Back to the list of Issue Briefs, *Volume 2, Number 1 (January 2001).*

SPEAKING

A. With the help of the notes that you made, study the table below. What do you think was the effect of such chemicals on the experimental animals mentioned below? Discuss this question with your partner. The teacher may ask you to present your findings to the class.

Chemicals that upset normal physiological processes

year	place	chemical	researcher	animal	effect
1981	University of California, Davis	DDT	—	male gulls	developed abnormal gonads that were more like ovaries than testes (feminised reproductive tract)
1992	Florida's Lake Apopka	DDT	Louis Guillette (zoologist)	drop in testosterone levels	male alligators
1992	Florida's Lake Apopka	DDT	Louis Guillette (zoologist)	higher than average estrogen levels	female alligators
1995	Henderson Minnesota	pesticide/ excessive vitamin-like chemicals	school children	frogs with five legs	frogs
1995	Henderson Minnesota	pesticide/ excessive vitamin-like chemicals	school children	extra eye near foreleg	frogs

B. With the help of a friend, discuss the impact that such chemicals can have on other animals and human beings.

You may be asked to present the results of your discussion to the whole class.

Activity 2

BEFORE YOU SPEAK

With the help of a partner, read the following extract from *The Hindu* (May 5, 2002) and make notes. You will need these notes when you play either the role of interviewer or environmentalist, later on in this lesson.

Added risks from dirty water

The widespread contamination of well water with arsenic in China and India has been linked to cancer and Blackfoot disease, which brings on gangrene in the foot and legs.

Now a new study from Taiwan points to another worry: drinking such water for two decades triples the risk of developing obstructions in the arteries leading to the brain, a danger sign for strokes and heart attacks.

In the study, published last month in the journal *Circulation*, researchers from National Taiwan University looked at 463 people in an area that formerly drew its water largely from contaminated wells.

The average arsenic level there was above 300 parts per billion; the Environmental Protection Agency last year reduced allowable levels in the United States from 50 parts per billion to 10 parts per billion.

For the study, the researchers divided the subjects into three groups based on how much arsenic they had encountered over the years and used ultrasound tests to look for arteriosclerosis.

People in the top third – those who had used the contaminated water for drinking and cooking for 20 years or more – had a risk three times as great as those in the bottom third.

The middle group had a risk twice as great as the bottom group.

'More than 100 million people are exposed to underground water with high concentrations of arsenic,' said the study's lead author, Dr. Chih-Hao Wang, who called the problem, 'an emerging epidemic.'

SPEAKING

A. Imagine you are a reporter and that you are interviewing an environmentalist for your paper. This environmentalist is David Nelson who has worked on ground water pollution in the US. In pairs, decide who will be the reporter and who will be the environmentalist.

Make a list of all the pollutants that you have come across which poison groundwater. You can list them out with the help of your partner. Your teacher will ask you to read out the names of the pollutants that you have come across. Just remember that you can consult the notes you made while you read the newspaper report on groundwater poisoning as you interview the environmentalist or answer the interviewer's questions as the environmentalist.

B. Give yourself a name, provided it is not damaging to anyone.

Those playing the role of the environmentalist should call themselves David Nelson.

Interviewer [I]	Environmentalist [E]
Greet E and introduce yourself to E.	Respond to I's greeting and politely ask I how he would like to be helped.
Explain the purpose of this visit to E.	Express willingness to be interviewed.
First ask E about his experience in the field.	Tell I that you have more than 20 years of experience studying ground water pollution. You can also tell him that you have not only studied it in the USA, but also in other Asian countries such as China, Vietnam and so on, and that now you are in India to study the problem.
Now ask E about the different pollutants destroying water sources.	Orally list the pollutants that affect ground water.
Ask E which pollutant in his opinion was the most hazardous.	Provide a suitable answer.

Ask E for reasons for considering that pollutant most hazardous.	Again give reasons.
Ask E to mention a solution for the problem.	Talk about a solution that would be appropriate in the Indian context.
Ask E politely if he is planning to implement it in the country.	Answer appropriately.
Express gratitude to E for granting permission to interview him in spite of his busy schedule.	Express pleasure.
Take leave from E.	Acknowledge I's leave-taking and say your own goodbye.

C. Your teacher will play a tape of David Nelson's speech. Make notes as you listen. After you listen to the speech (you can ask the teacher to play the tape more than once), talk to your partner and find out if you spoke appropriately on the subject of water pollution in your interview.

Now work with another pair, A with C and B with D, and ask similarly for reactions and comments on what you said.

UNIT FIVE

Reading

BEFORE YOU READ

Work in pairs to do this activity.

At some time or other, all of us would have looked at stars either with the naked eye or with the help of a telescope. Talk to your partner to decide which view is more satisfying, and why. In your discussion, take into account the experience of seeing very faint objects such as stars in the sky, and whether being able to see fine details is important.

READING

Read the following text and do the tasks which follow.

Optical telescopes

This month, Absolute Beginners *takes a look at some of the basic principles of the optical telescope, the most fundamental tool of astronomers.*

Iain Nicolson

The optical telescope is the fundamental instrument in the astronomer's armoury; it collects light from, and forms images of, distant objects. There are two principal types of telescope: the refractor, which uses a lens to collect light, and the reflector, which uses a mirror for the same purpose.

Forming an image

A refractor uses a convex lens called the objective, or object glass (OG), to collect light and form an image. Light from a distant point-like source (such as a star) arrives at the objective as parallel light rays. A ray of light entering the centre of the objective passes straight through without deviation while, because the surface of the lens is curved, the other rays are bent, or 'refracted', in such a way that they converge to a point—the focus of the lens—at which a point-like image of the distant star is formed. Rays of light from an object of finite angular size (such as the Moon, or a planet) form an inverted (upside-down) image of finite size.

A reflector uses a concave mirror—the primary mirror—in a similar way. The mirror is usually composed of a glass or ceramic material coated with a reflective metal (such as aluminium) on its front surface. Light reflected from this surface converges to form an image at a focus which is located in front of the mirror.

The clear diameter of the lens or mirror is its aperture (D); the distance between the centre of a lens, or the centre of the front surface of a mirror, and its focus is its focal length. The ratio of focal length to aperture (F/D) is called the focal ratio. The longer the focal length, the larger the image.

AN OPTICAL TELESCOPE FOR OBSERVATIONS

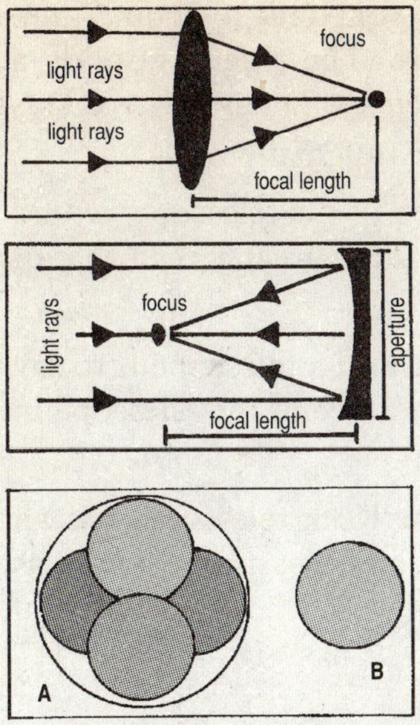

LIGHT GRASP

One of the main functions of a telescope is to collect more light than the unaided human eye can do and hence reveal objects which are too faint to be seen with the eye alone. The amount of light collected by a lens or a mirror is proportional to its surface area: the greater the surface area the greater the amount of light that will enter the telescope. Since the surface area of a circle is proportional to the square of its diameter, the light grasp of a telescope is proportional to the square of its aperture (D^2). If one telescope has an aperture twice as large as another, the light grasp of the larger will be four times the light grasp of the smaller ($2^2 = 4$).

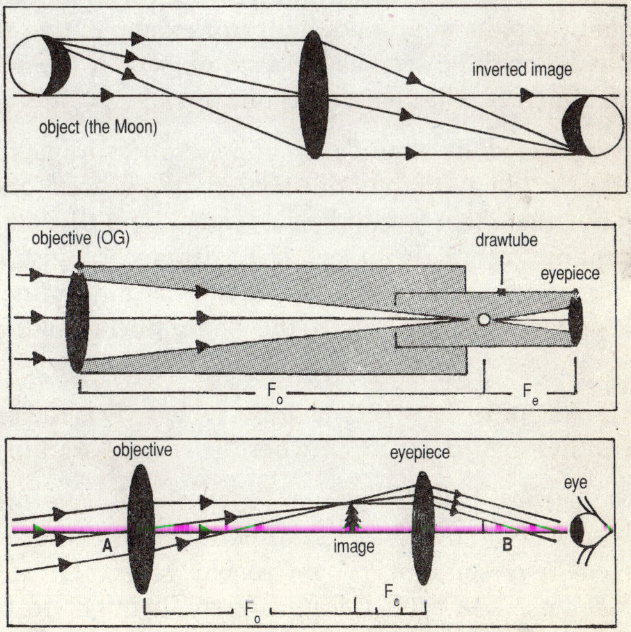

TOP: IMAGE FORMATION BY A LENS; MIDDLE: THE BASIC COMPONENTS OF A REFRACTOR; BOTTOM: MAGNIFICATION; RAYS FROM TOP AND BOTTOM OF AN OBJECT OF APPARENT SIZE A ENTER THE OBJECTIVE AND EMERGE FROM THE EYEPIECE AT ANGLE B. THE MAGNIFICATION IS B/A AND IS EQUAL TO F_O/F_E
(A REPRODUCTION OF AN GRAPHICS BY MARK MC LELLAN)

The aperture of the pupil of the human eye (d_e) expands to about 7 mm when it is fully adapted to dark conditions. The light grasp of a telescope, compared to the human eye, is given by $(D/d_e)^2$, where D is the aperture of the telescope and d_e is the aperture of the eye.

If D were one metre (1000 mm), the light grasp of the telescope would be $(1000/7)^2$, which is approximately 20,000 times greater than that of the eye.

One way, therefore, of describing the light grasp of a telescope is to say that light-grasp=20,000 D^2, where D is the aperture of the telescope in metres.

The largest optical telescope in the world, the Keck telescope, has an aperture of ten metres and so collects two million times as much light as the unaided human eye.

Resolving power

The resolving power of a telescope (R) is a measure of its ability to reveal fine details. It is usually defined in terms of the minimum angle by which two identical point sources of light (for example, two stars) must be separated in order to be seen as separate objects; if the angle is any smaller, the two images will merge into one.

R is usually expressed in seconds of angular measurement (arcsec), where one arcsec = one sixtieth of one sixtieth of a degree (one arcsec is equivalent to the angle that would be subtended by a £1 coin, which is about two centimetres in diameter, at a distance of just over four kilometres). Since we are interested in seeing as much fine detail as possible, the smaller the value of R the better the resolution of the telescope.

As an approximate guide, R = 120/ D arcsec, where D is the aperture of the telescope in millimetres (0.12/D, where D is expressed in metres).

A telescope of aperture 120 mm (about 5 inches) will have a theoretical resolving power of about one arcsec and should be able to distinguish as separate objects two stars of roughly-equal brightness if they are separated by at least one arcsec. Equivalently, it ought to be able to reveal craters larger than two kilometres in diameter on the surface of the Moon. By contrast, the theoretical resolution of the Keck telescope (10 m aperture) is 0.012 arcsec (equivalent to seeing a crater just over 20 metres in diameter on the Moon).

In practice, turbulence in the Earth's atmosphere causes star images to shimmer and shake and smears them out to such an extent that large telescopes on good sites seldom achieve resolutions much better than one arcsec. Even the best instruments at the best sites can only attain, at best, 0.25 arcsec unless sophisticated techniques are employed to compensate for the effects of the atmosphere. Consequently, although a larger telescope will always reveal fainter objects than a smaller one, it will not always reveal more detail.

The largest optical telescope in the world, the Keck telescope, has an aperture of ten metres and so collects two million times as much light as the unaided eye.

The Hubble Space Telescope has a 2.4 metre mirror—a quarter of the aperture of the largest ground-based instruments—but, because it is located in space clear of the degrading effects of the atmosphere, it operates to its theoretical limit of about 0.12/2.4 = 0.05 arcsec, about 5 times better than the best ground-based instrument can achieve.

From: Astronomy Now, *August 1997.*

[Iain Nicolson is a visiting Fellow of the University of Hertfordshire and a contributing consultant to Astronomy Now.*]*

AFTER YOU READ

A. 1. Work in pairs. A should ask B to say what the main difference between the two principal types of telescope is. B should reply, and then ask A to name the two types of telescope.

2. B should now ask A to say what the other name of a concave mirror is. A should respond and, in turn, ask B to give her the ratio between focal length and the size of the image a telescope forms.

B. Work by yourself. Read the text again if necessary to find out why, when the human eye collects light just as telescopes do, it is only through the telescope that we are able to see objects that are too faint to be seen by the human eye. Write this in the form of a note.

C. Work in pairs. A should ask B to explain how a telescope can display moon craters that are two kilometres in diameter. B should respond, and in turn ask A to explain how it is possible to view a moon crater that has a diameter of only 20 metres. Write down your answers.

D. Work in groups of three to decide if large telescopes can reveal finer details about stars. Write down a possible answer. Your teacher will ask you for the answers you have arrived at in C and D.

Writing and speaking

A. 1. List the names of some pests that attack plants and crops.

2. Work as a whole class. Your teacher will ask you to name some pesticides you know, and how these are used.

3. Your teacher will now look at how instructions are written. S(he) will ask you for suggestions on how instructions can be written in sequential order, and will put up the basic structure of a typical instruction [verb+obj and/or verb+complement etc.] on the board.

S(he) will then show you a set of pictures which show how pesticides are used and will ask you to list the key words you need to describe the actions in the pictures, and the names of the objects. (S)he will help with words you may not know such as *power sprayer, shoulder harness, gloves* and *mask*.

4. Work with your teacher and, using the grammar and vocabulary you have just looked at, frame a set of instructions based on the pictures on page 53.

B. This is a role-play activity.

1. Use the pictures your teacher has shown you in task (A) above. Imagine that you are officers in the Agricultural Centre, and choose one of these roles to play. One of them is that of the Agricultural Extension Officer talking to a cultivator or farmer. The other is that of the Public Relations Officer who wants to speak to a group of children about safety in the use of pesticides. Your teacher will help you understand the nature of your roles.

2. Prepare for your roles. The Agricultural Extension Officer (AEO) must write out a set of instructions on using pesticides, based on the pictures in task (A). The AEO will also need to prepare to translate these instructions into the local language. The Public Relations Officer (PRO) must write a short paragraph for the children's column of a newspaper on safety norms to be observed in the use of pesticides. For the role-play, the PRO must prepare to speak to a group of children.

3. Your teacher will work with you and help you finalise what you have written and what each of you will say in your separate roles as AEO and PRO.

4. Your teacher will now ask you to enact the role-play, separately for the AEO and the PRO.

C. Sometimes, a motorcycle has to be housed down for long periods when it is not in use. In such conditions, we need to know how to ensure that it is stored correctly. Look at the following

DO'S AND DON'TS IN USING PESTICIDES

instructions and checklist. Convert the table into a set of instructions for motorcycle owners.

	part(s)	activity
1.	fuel tank fuel lines carburettor float bowl	draining the fuel draining the fuel draining the fuel
2.	empty fuel tank	removing the fuel
3.	a cup of Servo super 30 oil	pouring into tank and shaking it to coat inner surfaces thoroughly, and draining excess oil
4.	spark plug	removing it and pouring one tablespoon of Servo super 30 oil in spark plug hole, and reinstalling it
5.	ignition	putting it off and kicking the engine over several times to coat cylinder walls with oil
6.	drive chain	removing it and cleaning it thoroughly with solvent and lubricating it with lubricants re-installing it or storing it in a plastic bag (tied to the frame for safe-keeping)
7.	control cables	lubricating them
8.	frame wheels	blocking up the frame to raise both wheels off the ground
9.	exhaust pipe	tying a plastic bag over it to prevent moisture from entering
10.	battery	removing it and charging it: storing it in a dry place and re-charging it once a month

PREPARING TO SPEAK

A. In groups of four or five, work out a plan for a one-day science exhibition in your college. To prepare for this, first study the list of items below. As you read and talk about the list of items, write YES in the box if the item is important for the plan and NO if the item is not important.

No.	Checklist	YES / NO
1.	who to ask permission from to hold the exhibition, and when to ask for it	☐
2.	deciding who the visitors will be (e.g., which colleges to invite, which professional bodies to send out	☐

invitations to, which government officials to invite and so on) and deciding when to send out the invitations

3. estimating the budget and drawing up a proposal to submit to the college authorities for receiving the money. The budget will probably cover advertising (including the charges for printing the invitations), local hospitality for visiting dignitaries, travel expenses for the organisers, day-to-day expenses until the day of the event, extra funding that would cover the cost of hiring a power generator (in case of power failures), electricity charges, the cost of special equipment such as the OHP (the overhead projector), multimedia computers, cost of setting up the booths, the refreshment area, and so on.
4. advertising the event in the media—the local dailies, All India Radio, wall posters, hand bills, via e-mail, science exhibition website, and so on
5. budgeting for and arranging for accommodation, food, and an allowance for each of the organisers (student volunteers) for a week until the day of the event
6. providing for refreshments for the delegates during events such as seminars and demonstrations
7. asking for student volunteers who would be assistants to demonstrators, ushers, timekeepers, caretakers of visitors' things, errand boys and so on
8. hiring a chef for preparing an exhibition dinner that evening
9. requesting the local police station for a few constables to prevent rowdy students from disturbing the peace
10. inviting the local politician, police commissioner, the magistrate, or the head of a corporate body to inaugurate the event
11. inviting an educationist, the secretary of a prominent college, or the vice-chancellor of the local university for the valedictory ceremony
12. requesting the municipal authorities to deploy sanitary workers to clean up the college neighbourhood

13.	planning to meet prospective sponsors (usually prominent businessmen, hoteliers, philanthropists and so on) who would provide the funding needed for running the event	☐
14.	organising a press meet at the end of the event	☐
15.	requesting the local transportation authorities to run a few specials (extra buses for visiting students)	☐
16.	budgeting for buying gifts and mementos for the guests	☐
17.	asking college authorities for space to hold the exhibition	☐
18.	soliciting help from students' associations such as the photography club, philately club, NCC, National Social Service (volunteers), first aid club, fine arts club, astronomy club, rock climbing club, nature club, book review club, the drama club, the literary club and so on to run the event	☐
19.	soliciting help from the local university researchers to help out with scientific experiments, abstract explanations and so on.	☐

SPEAKING

A. In small groups of four or five, choose a topic in the project of organising a science exhibition. Some of the topics you can choose are budgeting, organising transport, refreshments and seeking help from other departments. As you discuss the topic you have chosen, one of the members of your group will have to make a checklist. Now choose a topic for discussion and discuss it for about seven minutes.

B. Following the discussion, look at some of the ground rules and see if you followed them.

Did you and the members of your group get equal chances to take part in the discussion? For example, were there any members in your group who were doing all the talking and keeping the others from taking part in the discussion? Was there any member who was not taking part in the discussion at all?

Here are some criteria for evaluating your contribution. Give yourself 2 points for every 'positive' answer (see the parts in boldface) and 1 point for every answer which indicates that you were not following the rules.

		Points
1.	**Were you speaking for just as long as you should have**—that is, not for so long that others in the group became impatient, or not so briefly that it was obvious that there was more to be said?	
2.	**Were you contributing to the discussion,** that is, not staying silent?	
3.	**Were you responding in phrases or sentences, or in yes–no monosyllables?**	
4.	**Were you giving other members a chance to contribute**—that is, were you talking at such length that others were not able to say what they wanted to say?	
5.	**Were you keeping to the point** (or were you talking about everything else except the topic of discussion)?	
6.	**Were you watchful about tone and volume?** (Do you talk either too loud, thereby distracting others, or in whispers so that listeners had to strain to understand what you were saying?)	

Use the score you have to correct any aspects which show that you could improve your role as a member of the group.

C. Now choose another topic for discussion, for example, taking help from other departments. Try to remember the rules you have just seen.

You may want to complete the table below when you are about halfway through the discussion. It will help you keep track of turn-taking in discussions.

Evaluate your role as honestly as you can. If you answered YES to any of the questions below, give yourself a point.

		Points
1.	Are you able to intervene appropriately when another member is speaking, and take over from her/him? In other words, do you move in easily to carry forward the discussion or do you keep waiting for the other member to stop talking?	

2.	Are you able to intervene smoothly without annoying the member who is speaking, or do you interrupt her or him and cause some unpleasant feelings?	
3.	Are you able to signal verbally that you are ready to take your turn, (for example, 'You have a point there, but if I may differ with you...') or do you make coughing noises or shift around to distract the person who is speaking and then take your turn?	
4.	Do you signal that you are closing or do you usually come to a dead stop, that is, stop speaking abruptly? In other words, do you use words and phrases to indicate that your turn is coming to an end (e.g. 'And, a good budget, *all said and done*, is only a tool in the hands of people. It is only the person who gives life to a budget.')?	
5.	In situations when you have not finished and another member wants to come in, do you indicate that your turn is still not finished or do you assert yourself by, for example, speaking louder than usual and cutting the person off?	
6.	In turn, do you stop trying to move in when the one who is speaking indicates that he/she has not finished?	
7.	How do you enter the discussion politely when another member is speaking? Do you, for example, say something like *'If I may add another point to what you've just been saying...'*?	

Use your score to evaluate yourself and to improve your role as a member of the group. With a partner, count the total number of points that you have earned so far. If you have scored more than seven points in each case (in the two sessions above), then you can be assured that your discussion skills are improving. If they are below seven, it definitely means that you have to improve; you need to work on the different sub-skills of speaking that will help you to become a better contributor in discussions.

D. Work as a whole class with your teacher to discuss the points that came up in the course of pair work and group work sessions. Use the discussion to reflect on the skills you have learnt as well as your role as a learner.